How to Accept

Trust & Live

Your Life's

Spiritual Purpose

Am I Worthy?

Brent Atwater

Just Plain Love® Books
inspiring thoughts that provide smiles, hugs and healing for every reader's heart!

This *Just Plain Love*® Book
is given

To: _____

Message: _____

_____

with
LOTS of LOVE
and
HUGS!!!

From:

_____

Date:

_____

Published and Distributed in the United States by:

Just Plain Love® Books, Brent Atwater
www.BrentAtwater.com   or www.JustPlainLoveBooks.com

Editorial: Brent Atwater   Cover Design: Brent Atwater
Interior Design: Brent Atwater   Illustrations: Brent Atwater

The author of this book, Brent Atwater, is not a medical doctor nor
associated with any branch of allopathic medicine. Brent is a Holistic
Integrative Energy Medicine specialist in Medical Intuitive Diagnosis.
ALWAYS consult a physician or trained health care professional either
directly or indirectly concerning any physical or medical problem or condition
before undertaking any diet, health related technique or lifestyle change
program.

The contents presented herein are derived from the author's intuition
and experiences. The intent of the author is only to offer information of a
general nature to help facilitate your journey to health and well-being. In the
event you choose to use any of the information in this book for yourself,
which is your constitutional right, as in traditional medicine, there are no
guarantees and the author and the publisher assume no responsibility for your
actions.

Library of Congress Cataloging-in-Publication Data
ISBN-10: 0615581919
ISBN-13: 9780615581910
Hardcover ISBN:
Kindle ASIN: B004OR1NU6
Ebook ISBN 978-1-4524-8656-7
Audio Book:
R2

This book is translated into other languages and available in print
and eBooks at most online retailers.

R 2012

USA Canada France, UK, AU, SA Japan check with other distributor s
Publisher's Price Higher in Other Countries

Acknowledgements

I want to thank all of those who have supported and encouraged my journey and the authors, speakers and teachers who contributed to shaping my consciousness. Special thanks to Michael Wellford, Charles Nunn and my beloved pets for their contributions and enduring patience with my spiritual path.

I also want to thank you the reader for taking your time to explore my books and for allowing me to share what I have learned and am learning. It is my intent and hope that this information will facilitate better health, greater perspectives, expanded awareness and knowledge for balance, well being enjoyment and wonderful memories in your life. A special thanks to Meg Martin for her inexhaustible supply of patience and attention to details and to Maude or Myrtle for their support and tenaciousness.

Dedication

To Thomas Michael Ramseur Wellford, whose life, love and passing made my understanding possible. I shall always hold you and hear you in my heart, my soul and my dreams.
To those very special people and pets who have been my joy, with whom I have shared hope, laughter and LIFE!!!

Special Gratitude

To all my "voices" and guides and the other energies and entities who serve the Christ White Light named and unnamed who were relentless, impatient, persistent, exhausting, exasperating, informative, accurate, edgy, humorous, entertaining, deliberate, persuasive, detailed beyond belief and always of the highest integrity and utmost determination for me and my clients" highest and best good.
I admire their patience with my path, their directives for my education and evolution and their ongoing and forever training of my soul.
They are my best friends, greatest teachers, constant companions, best protectors, collaborators and support team.
Namaste! Et al Y"all ☺

Table of Contents

Everything you ever need to learn,
see or know resides inside of you!

Your job is to choose, trust, protect,
cleanse and allow the Gift to flow through you

Introduction

I love MIDI and the science of medical intuitive diagnosis! I love looking into each client"s body. To me, each body is a wonderful theater providing a unique view of each and every play in all the stages of an individual"s life!

I"m amazed at what it the human body can do, how it functions, regenerates and how it readapts to life altering situations right before my eyes.

Since I have no medical training to color my opinions and affect my findings I KNOW there is a God and a Universal Higher Power connection when I use my gift. I approach every new experience with accountability, humility and appreciation for the blessed responsibility of my Gifts.

Seeing medical disease and disorders so graphically within each human or animal shows me how health can alter your life. So I focus on how my Gift benefits others. It provides accurate insight, information and intuitive directives that facilitate each soul"s healing journey.

Sitting in my office, I can mentally see (like a MRI film) the cancer ridden intestinal sac of a woman in the Philippines that I have never met. Or I might be looking at the disconnected cranial nerve in a client"s brain in Greece that is causing her double vision and seizures.

Watching the heartbeat monitor of a child stabilize under my directive gaze thousands of miles away or having a client report the bleeding has stopped, the respiration rate has steadied or the oxygen levels are raising when clients are more than half way around the world is irrefutable proof to me that there is a Higher Power!   No matter how many times I see these awesome things and am given the privilege of participating, it"s humbles me!

I offer my experience to each holistic integrative energy medicine professional, intuitive healer, educator, researcher, spiritual purpose seeker, student, dreamer and curious reader from my soul"s "experiences."

My intent is to facilitate, teach and empower student"s innate skills to the level that God has intended their soul to experience in this lifetime.

Your Gift was created for your contributions. You are uniquely created to perform what YOU came to contribute. Your gift''s worth is not one iota less or more important than anyone else. We all serve humanity with our different skills.

The information presented in this book will not interfere with what you do or with any intuitive or healing modalities. These tools and techniques will most likely awaken, enhance, amplify and expand your current abilities.

Use only that information which resonates with your soul.

the Journey Begins

The phone rings and a client halfway across the globe, asks to speak to Brent Atwater, Medical Intuitive. I answer the phone. The client is surprised when they get me. I presume they would like to speak with the person they want to work with.

The caller asks if I can evaluate what has stymied their physician. I explain that my X ray vision shows me every organ, tissue, bone, brain area, nerves, cells and all the body systems.

With that visual information, I am able to answer their questions about what, where and how intense their health issues are. I intuitively suggest where to tell their healthcare professionals to look and what tests to take. I furnish medical words so they can discuss these concepts or areas with their doctor. I also relate that I can look at their future energy for prognosis.

Since every individual's energy contains a timeline. I follow, "track," interpret and diagnose a person's energy from prebirth into the future.

This book is presented in the order that I learned. Perhaps it will seem familiar and make your awakening less confusing or illuminate a place within your soul that is vaguely familiar. It is my intent and hope that this will ignite all that you are and can be, or at the very least provoke some interesting thoughts and questions.

I was in the original study group for Extra Sensory Perceptions (ESP) tested by Dr. J. B. Rhine from Duke University at age 5.

We loved the days when "the men in the white lab coats" would come and play mind games with me and my classmates in another building. We played guess the dominos and number sequences. We guessed what our classmates were doing, writing or thinking. It was fun.

Our school group was considered "gifted." We became the pilot program that provided the guidelines for Governor Terry Sanford's national "Gifted Program" for grades 1 -12

Throughout our "special" education, one of the most fascinating concepts was introduced in our freshman year.

We were told that due to our heightened sensitivity, there were those of us who might not be able to handle all of our sensory input. We were taught how to disconnect from our mind"s chatter so it wouldn"t disrupt our daily lives.

Later in college, I learned several of my most brilliant high school class mates committed suicide. After that I mastered how to shut down my thoughts when I wanted to and practiced it regularly!

Growing up, I thought that seeing energy was normal and listening to intuition about everything was what everyone did. Example, at one point after purchasing a new home, when I would come near the toilet I"d hear the word "septic tank." The only way to cease my inner guidance was to do something about the subject matter. So I called a company, explained that I had just moved into a new home and knew nothing about septic tanks. I asked would they please send someone out to check the septic system.

As soon as the man completed his work, he informed me "Lady, if you had not called us today, your septic system"s contents would have backed up into your bathtub and all your sinks."

THANK YOU inner guidance! I NEVER discount and **always** act on the advice that I am given even regarding septic tanks!

In 1997 my beloved best friend and fiancé Michael Wellford was killed in an unexpected automobile crash. Several days after his death, ALL my Gifts exploded full front and center and were driving me crazy.

Regress for a moment. Actually the Gift started before Mike left on Easter Sunday. The last thing I said to him was "Mikey, please don't drive down here next weekend, you are so tired you're gonna kill yourself in that car!" Little did I know my inner guidance was giving me a "heads up."

Friday night, I talked to Mike on the phone at 6:30 pm. He said he would be arriving at 9:30 pm. At 9:30 I was having excruciating pains in my chest to the point of calling a friend and asking her to keep talking to me until Mike arrived in case I needed to go to the emergency room. About 9:45, the pain subsided and I got off the phone by telling her "I'll just wait till Mike arrives any minute now."

Unbeknownst to me, Mike had fallen asleep at the wheel and was in a car wreck around 9:30. The steering wheel went through his chest and he died about 9:45 pm.

After the funeral I went to Duke University Medical Center and sat in the waiting room determined to meet the head of the Integrative Medical Center. A man popped his head around a corner after hour 6.5 and asked who I wanted to see. After I told him, he stated, "I,,m Dr. Larry Burk, you're looking for me!"

I told him what was happening. He immediately took me into a freshman class of his x-ray students and asked me what was wrong with each person's x-ray displayed on the room's huge wall monitors. Information just spilled out of me like I knew what I was doing. I didn't. I had no medical education or degree as I majored in creative writing and art at Hollins University and then attended Wake Forest University Law School.

Of note: Prior to this occurring, my friends always thought it was funny that I was mesmerized by the *New England Journal of Medicine* and the *Journal of the American Medical Association, Prevention* and any and all other health informative magazines were my favorite things to read for leisure.

21

You'll learn later that inexplicable deep seated interests like this are known to your soul; even though these interests are not in flow with the life you are currently living (I was modeling in New York.)

Dr. Burk sent me home with a list of books to read and told me I was a "medical intuitive." I had never heard those words before although they were soon to shape my destiny.

After Mike was killed, my life was blown apart. To provide hope for my future, friends arranged a reading for me with an internationally renowned intuitive. During that reading she told me that I was going to "channel information," I had no idea what that meant. She also relayed that I would be able to see inside of human body like Superman's x-ray vision. Right!

A few days later I told a friend about the intuitive "reading." He said "OK, then look at my heart." So I said out loud, "I ask to see his heart." The next thing I knew, there all bright red and shiny superimposed over his body was his pumping heart with all the moving valves and his entire coursing vascular system. I turned pale white and got so sick at my stomach that I had to sit down on the ground to avoid passing out! What was happening to me!?????????????????

I hid out in my room for several days afraid to deal with any more visuals like that again. Then I remembered the inituitive's predictions and decided to learn what she meant by "channel" and "see inside" bodies. I began my quest to LEARN what I was doing. And more importantly <u>how to control it</u>!

It took **many** years, multiple techniques, a lot of testing and ongoing personal mental control and verbal command tools to learn how to harness, understand, direct and guide this magnificent Gift for the benefit of others. Otherwise this awesome ability called a "Gift" by some, a power by others and just plain weird by even more, would use me up and dominate my life.

In my seminars, workshops, training programs etc, I describe it like this: My Gift is a beautiful wonderful amazing wild stallion that is incredibly powerful. Either you learn how to ride and harness the stallion at YOUR direction and know when to put him back into the stable and lead a normal life, or that stallion will dominate and exhaust you and your life.

The Universe provided me with a Gift that activated when I wanted to "just do it!"

I needed no training or certifications other than listening to Guidance. This was incredible stuff to deal with!

I found that even though the Gift isolated me, it gave me a higher connection. I learned 99% of all I know from asking the "voices in my head" to "show me" and provide the information and answers I need.

I hope that you enjoy reading about my journey. I have tried to write it as if you are sitting in my presence having a conversation. My way of teaching is storytelling. All I know is what I"ve experienced. I hope my journey provides insight, clarity and assistance for your path.

I have found that all of my book"s ideas and concepts about living with a Gift of intuitive healing energy and medical intuition boil down to a simple theory and 5 assignments:

GO with who you are, BE who you are. Don"t let the lack of knowledge, anything or anyone tell YOU, about what YOU KNOW!

If you are truly a conduit, JUST BE ONE!!

The Universe and God will do the rest!

Everything that you ever need to learn, see or know about your life's spiritual purpose resides inside of you.

Your assignment is to:

1. Choose, accept, trust, protect, cleanse and allow the Gift to flow through you.

2. Show up with accountability, responsibility and integrity.

3. Follow the directives of your Higher Power and Guides and trust the information given to you.

4. Detach remove and release from your client and session. Go onto your next experience unfettered and unaffected by energy, issues or entities.

5. Go home and enjoy your life on earth!

Everything you
ever need to learn,
see or know,
resides
inside of you!

A "Gift"

Finding your spiritual purpose is sometimes a life journey, other times an unfolding process or simply a choice to use what you've been given.

So you think that you may have a "Gift." Maybe you were born knowing that you had special talents or people told you that you are "gifted." Perhaps life provided sudden change that awakened talents within you that had been simmering or previously asleep. Now your soul's yearning is pointing you in a new life direction, persistently amplifying a feeling you just can't shake! Sometimes you may feel isolated and think you're just "weird" or "crazy," but inherently you "know" that you're Ok. You may feel "different" and always have, but you understand what is different in you is good!

A Gift can also be initiated with an inexplicable and sudden redirection of your life through an event. Sometimes when you're a success in your job or life, you may experience a medical situation, a debilitating event or an unexpected loss. It's a moment in time that alters and rearranges everything and changes your relationship to everyone in your life.

After that experience, you begin to be drawn towards a spiritual purpose. You discover the emergence of new Gifts. It's the Universe directing your path to your soul's contract.

Since a Gift can wreak havoc with all areas of your being, I'm going to try to break it down to what most people question.

Always remember that your Gift will never be static unless you just shut down. Even then, God, the Universe or your Higher Power will be working in unforeseen ways. Gifts always evolve.

You may begin on one path and experience many different avenues throughout your life. Caution, don't get so locked into a specific direction that you miss guidance that is leading you towards greater possibilities.

Remember you are a spiritual being in a human body learning in the earth school. Your entire life process is your soul's journey. Your choices navigate and create the consequences throughout that adventure.

Let's start with the mental aspects. You have free will choice. You have a CHOICE to use your Gift in this incarnation. You can accept or reject your Gifts by free will choice and/or set some or all of them aside for another embodiment.

However if you have agreed to be a
_____, then your soul has a
contractual obligation to fulfill with the
Universe /Higher Power.

Don't be a healer, intuitive, animal
communicator or whatever your Gift may
embody because a reading "told you so."
Don't use your Gift because your ego wants
to do so. (Then the Gift is already "tainted,"
more about that later) Be open to your soul's
contract because it's your heart's desire and
your soul's knowing.

If you grew up as a child with your Gift, you
are in what they call the Contract A group,
using your special talents early in life. Those
of us that had Gifts activated later in life are
the contract B activation group according to
www.Lightworker.com archives.

Why would you not accept your Gifts?
You are not required to use all of your Gifts.
Use only those Gifts that resonate and create
happiness while you use them. Just because
you have lots of clothes in a closet, you don't
have to wear them all at once. Neither do you
have to experience and use all your Gifts at
once.

Since you are in charge of your body and Gifts, choose the specific Gift(s) that you are addressing and the timeframe in which you want to use it, or not. You get to set the parameters of your Gifts involvement in your life.

Prayer for the Gifts you want to shut down:

Say: Thank you for the Gift of _____. I choose not to use _____ (name the Gift) at _____ (this time or choose a time frame, or in this incarnation) unless it for my highest and best good and protection. So be it. It is done! Thank you.

Deciding to use your Gift-

How do you know what you'll be doing with it? Usually the random interests that you have been drawn to throughout your life are part of your calling. Additionally, every bit of "training" that you have experienced up to this point will fuel the direction or focus of what you"ll do. Example, if you were a drug addict, or always liked animals, or were drawn to flowers, usually the culmination of all your experiences will provide the training for your client base.

Many times you"ll work in a setting with the type of individuals that you have been around all your life. Your background in society, career, karmic path, environmental conditions and previous issues that you have dealt with are all preparation for your work with the exact type of individuals who have issues that you have experienced. Your personal tests, testimonials and experiences have trained you for your specific clientele.

The Universe has spent a great deal of time educating you for your purpose, so what you"ve done is a large contributing factor to who, where, when and what type of client base will benefit from your service.

As examples: affluent individuals usually have contacts because they can relate to one another"s lifestyle. A recovered alcoholic usually is the best AA mentor. A homeless man or ex con works well within their experiential community. All come to serve through their life choice lessons.

What you considered a medical hardship, social dysfunction, or being "bad" was Universe training 101. Everything that was "horrific" or an accelerated course was designed to prime you for graduate school exams!

Anything you ever experienced was Universe University"s preparation for you to live your spiritual purpose.

There will come a time when everything that you have ever done or participated in will make sense and "jell." If you were a "wild" child and now have a calling, you"ll probably be working with women who are in the same situation that you were involved in and have grown through. So review your past history of learning; the good, bad and ugly. That information will usually provide the clearest directives most appropriate for your purpose.

On the other hand, you may wake up one morning, change your mind and jump start a brand new direction for your life. Your soul"s guidance will always prevail.

Prayer to help focus your path:
Say: I ask and it is my intent to bring in any and all people who will benefit from my Gifts and service to others and to close the doors and remove all people that do not accelerate my spiritual purpose for my highest and best good. Thank you, so be it, it is done.

This prayer comes with a warning, be VERY careful for what you ask for!

Please read this twice:

No client base or spiritual purpose or path is more important than another; it's just your assignment for this incarnation.

The individuals serving kings and queens, those serving the homeless, working for free and the highly paid are all equal in the Universe"s eyes. Each just has a different territory, assignment and pay scale for the relative client base served. Your Gift is unique to you and your service. If we all were the same then humanity"s needs would have to be the same. Gifts come in various strengths and flavors to meet multiple needs.

The Emotional Side of the Gift

You"ve made the decision that you *are* going to accept your calling in this incarnation or a portion thereof.

All of a sudden doubts set in. Why do I feel so alone? Why do I feel so isolated and different when I"m supposed to be so lovingly in service to others? Am I good enough? Will I ever be good enough? Am I worthy? I"m afraid I might misuse my Gift. What if I do misuse my Gift?

35

Ok, if I accept this Gift, is this real? What do I do with what I have? There has to be downsides! How in the world will I ever be able to support myself doing this? Am I supposed to support myself with my Gift? Why are there so many changes in the people around me now?

Why does my life feel like it"s turning upside down? Why are long standing relationships changing? What did I do to my family and friends to make them so unsupportive or dismissive about my Gifts? What if I"m on the wrong spiritual path? How can I find out WHAT path I"m supposed to be on? These are the most frequently asked questions that plague "newbies!" Let"s examine them one at a time.

Personal Isolation: You are not alone in spirit, your energy has shifted. You will be reconnecting with a new frequency. You feel detached, because you are not "feeling" your world, family and friends and others in the old familiar energy pattern.

Gifted people must learn to stand in their own power and emotionally alone in order to trust their own intuition.

Often they have come from a dysfunctional or very detached family, unusual friends and a unique environmental background or from other surrounding circumstances that create and require them to trust their own gut reactions just to get where they are in their current life.

Think about it, if there was a world catastrophe and you were affected by everything and listened to everyone"s opinion, how could you find the time to make a great decision and trust how best to serve under those pressing conditions? On the other hand if you listened to your Higher Power and your guidance, the solution would be truly Divine and your direction pure.

When my Goddaughter was born with status epileptic seizures, at one point I was called to stabilize her heart rate and breathing while she awaited a Life Flight. When I went into the room there was a tiny fragile human being with more wires and monitors on her than there was body weight. I was so distraught, that I had to leave the room due to nausea and to keep my knees from collapsing with grief and concern. At that moment, I was absolutely NO help to her because my human emotions engulfed and overrode my Gift.

Right then and there I decided I needed to "shake off" my emotional feelings and go in that room and do what I came to Earth to do. My job was to listen to, be directed by and trust my guidance so she could be healed.

I took a deep breath and marched myself back into that room while saying my prayers. I worked fervently for the next 15 minutes until her heartbeat stabilized and her pulmonary function restored to a normal range where it stayed as the Life Flight loaded her aboard.

After I knew she was safe, I went outside and cried. I learned the effectiveness of my Gift was diminished by getting caught up in my personal feelings about the circumstances and "situation."

It"s not that you can"t care about what is going on. I had to remove myself from having any expectations for the outcome to be a pure conduit of information and healing energy. If I allowed myself to have emotional expectations, I would have tainting or misinterpreted my Guidance"s directives.

You must learn to differentiate and discern how to be in and maintain an energy state when you listen **only** to God"s guidance for your Gift.

In time you will learn to embrace this solitary and oneness state. It will herald the onset of your empowerment with wonderful new service opportunities. Being in that "cocoon" is standing in your full power as a person, as the director of your life force energy and as a pure conduit.

Self esteem issues "I'm not worthy."

It doesn't matter! Read that again!

It doesn't matter!

YOU got **picked by God**, the Universe / your Higher Power!
Therefore you <u>are</u> the "Pickee!"

Let's clarify this concept

Who are YOU to question GOD's
/ the Universe"s/ Your Higher Power"s judgment about picking you since "**They**" **are omnipotent and all knowing**?

When you doubt, you're being conceited!
Are you actually inferring and basically telling
GOD that He has poor judgment,
made a mistake and
chose the incorrect person

when HE picked YOU!

Are YOU so omnipotent that YOU can tell
GOD that He was wrong in choosing you?

God feels you are worthy.
That's ALL you need to KNOW!

It doesn't matter WHY you are the
"Pickee."
You are!
**That's all you need to understand &
accept.**

Your designation is not going away in this
incarnation if you choose to use your Gift!

If you do NOT choose to use your Gift in this
life, you are still the "Pickee" until you have
fulfilled that "Pickee" contractual agreement
with the Universe/ Higher Power in this or
another incarnation.

I suggest you quit trying to fight being the "Pickee."

No matter what YOU think or feel. Since you ARE the "Pickee," decide this is the embodiment to shine!

I'm afraid I might misuse my Gift.

Even though you"ve sorta accepted being the "Pickee," you"re afraid of the responsibility of the Gift and its unknowns.

Have you ever thought that this might be the incarnation where you are the good guy and get to enjoy, be recognized for and celebrate what you have, rather than be burned, stoned or killed for those special talents?

An old sage told me not to feel afraid. I asked "why?"She said that whatever we feared was what we had already experienced in another life, which was why, it was such a strong feeling in this lifetime. WE know from a past life what the down side was.

Because we have ALREADY, key word, **already been through** the bad with our Gift in another lifetime, then we don"t have to go through that "learning opportunity" from our Gift again. Whew!

This incarnation we get to enjoy our Gift and use it as we so choose.   Her explanations resonated with me and eliminated my being "afraid of doing harm."

If you truly believe that every lifetime is an opportunity to learn experience and evolve for the next embodiment, then her insight will help you too.

How to use your Gift in complete Trust

Do you just halfway believe that all this is true and really happening? Are you in a stall pattern? Do you represent yourself to be a Light worker but are not really honoring yourself and your Gifts because of self doubt and lack of complete trust? If you answered "Yes," then you're diluting your purpose.

How old are you?? Let's pretend you are going to live to be 100. Now let's determine what percentage of your life you've already "used up" 45%, 60 %??
This is a reality check. At 50 you've used up 50%. Ask yourself: how are you going to use your Gift with the time you have left?

I suggest that since you've had a physical birthday for your body that you choose a date and designate it to be your soul's birthday.

Celebrate your soul's birthday each year like you do your physical birthday. Invite your friends. Make an announcement and create a support system for yourself.

On **your soul's birthday make a promise** to the Universe / God. Commit to and say out loud:
"I'll never live in half beliefs and "sorta Trust" any more. I choose to evolve and BE all I am and can be. I Live I AM, I TRUST!"

Halfway believing is like being half pregnant or saying I totally Trust except when I fly in airplanes.

**You must choose to give up worry 100%
You must choose to Trust 100%.**

It's a CHOICE, your choice of how to believe.

If not, you're shortchanging and diluting all that is available to you.

Declaration, affirmation and promise to empower your Trust:
Say: I choose to no longer misrepresent myself to myself and others. I choose to live and BE my soul's contract. I choose to trust and never go back to a lack of faith and self doubt from this moment forward. So be it, it is done!

So what do you say to people who falter? First, recognize that you fell back into your old thought/life pattern. Determine what made you regress and correct that pattern. Second, start over and say the affirmation again. Third move forward until you live it, no matter how many times you have to do it!

You'll be tested, count on it!
State to the test: "I've had my soul's birthday, I live in TRUST! Now, forever more and always!"

Think about it, do you really want to go back on your word to God?

If God/ the Universe / your Higher Power doesn't want you to do something they will stop you. Or provide enough free will choice failures that you will "get" that you are choosing the wrong pattern of actions.

Now you will be **progressing** on your spiritual path from a position of Trust, rather than just processing learning techniques and self doubt issues.

So far you"ve determined the Gifts you want to use and accepted using your Gift in this incarnation in full Trust.

How fast do you want to progress?

Since you"ve accepted your "assignment, don"t be surprised if your heart wants to help but you"re frustrated by not doing what you "feel you came here to do." You may like you are "wasting your life." "All my Gifts have not come together. I feel like I have spent my entire life struggling and I don"t know what I am doing." "I feel rejected by the Universe. I don"t get the positive feedback and support that I need to move forward." " I think I know what I"m doing, but how can I be sure this is my spiritual purpose?" "What am I supposed to do when I am in service?"

You get to direct your life forward
UNLESS the Universe wants you to do this RIGHT NOW!

I know a lady that was stuck in Canada with a car that needed to be repaired. She took a waitress job to pay for the car in order to continue on her trip.

One day she was talking with a customer who asked if she believed in "fortune telling" and she said yes. The customer said "why don"t you just tell me what you see in my future?" not expecting any results.

Information erupted out of her! The customer sat stunned at the accuracy of detail and knowledge about her life. The customer then went home and told another friend.

Within a week, this woman was giving 25 readings a day for free and was so tired she had to quit waitressing. Almost broke, she started charging for her readings and the rest of the story- she is a renowned international intuitive.

The Universe wanted her in service RIGHT NOW!!! If that is the case with you, "They" will provide absolutely everything that you need to do what you came here to do.

If you're not recruited into immediate service, your next choice is to monitor the speed of your progression or to accelerate it.

First, you need to honor your path. If you don't honor your path, why should anyone else.

Prayer to remove blocks in your life's and move forward in your spiritual purpose: **Say**: Send all the people and experiences to me now that will amplify my soul's purpose and open any and all doors for my highest and best good.   Remove any and all people, energy, entities, pledges, experiences, promises or any and all life commitments that hinder my path, now forevermore and always. So be it, it is done! Thank you!

Second, ask yourself if there is anything holding you back?

If you think you're "failing" or not moving forward on your path fast enough ask for Trust. Ask to be shown another way to go forward. Do not fold your tent; ask to be shown another way.

This is also "Their" way of teaching you to ask for directives, information and guidance in order for you to learn that you"ll get quickest results by going straight to THE source! A diverted direction by the Universe is a straight path to where you should be going.

Prayer for your soul's path and spiritual purpose

Say: I ask and it is my intent to close any and all doors, stop any and all activities, remove any and all energies and entities now and in all of time and all there is, that are not for my highest and best good and that are interfering and impeding my soul"s purpose. Direct me on my soul's path now. So be it it is done.

This prayer cuts the Karmic timing, "processing" and starts you living, being and progressing on your spiritual purpose. You will now BE, all you are and can be, not one iota less!!!!! Shine, shine, shine!

Third, since you are in the physical body you can always ask to accelerate or slow down your soul's journey.

Be very careful and ready for the unexpected when you ask for acceleration. Ask specifically for the type of acceleration that you want.

Say: I ask and it is my intent for the Universe to accelerate my path now or ____ make your request here ____ now. So be it, it is done.

I tested this theory one day while walking my dog. I asked for an acceleration of clients, the next day I had 23 + calls. Most of my sessions require 5 or more hours, which is different from an hourly appointment practice. So a few days later I chose to request that "They" hold off new clients for a while. They did! Then I told Them, "I'm ready to go back to work." And that's how I regulate the speed of my business unless I'm given a Higher Objective to complete within a specific timeframe assignment. I always trust that everything will work out and I'll get to rest at the appropriate time!

Of note: Once you establish a work and life path flow pattern, don't be overly concerned during a lull or a pause in your path. The Universe is lining up all the myriad details within your journey.

During the slow times you have an opportunity to do humanly chores, domestic errands and catch up on personal details and human life activities.

Then be prepared for more progressing on your path.

KNOW that after the lull, almost always the fast, full pace resumes.

Attitude: Gift versus Ego/ Power

Some people allude to having "powers." "Power" is ego thinking and taints the very energy that you channel. A lot of individuals claim their Gift to be a power not realizing they have just diminished their wattage by adding a filter of ego over their previously clear purpose. I suggest that you be the steward of your "Gift" that channels thru you rather than use your "Gift" as ego empowerment.

After all that decision making and choosing directives for your life the next phase is about responsibilities!

As the "Pickee"
your job is:
To choose, accept,
trust, protect,
cleanse and allow
the Gift
to flow through
you.

Responsibilities for the Life You Have Chosen

Your primary responsibility is divided into three categories: They are Protecting/ Shielding, Cleansing and Allowing.

Protecting yourself requires getting your prayers and intent on a specific tract. Let"s look at how to pray in order to carefully craft and direct your prayers.

How to Pray: Be SPECIFIC!

The Universe lives in forever time and your leased vehicle (body) lives in finite time, so you need to be very specific. Say:

I ASK: "ask and ye shall receive." It's a Universal Law that all those in charge of your soul's contract must respond. You're asking all those in charge of your soul to help you, now! Why not use ALL the powers you have on heaven and earth that are available to you???

It is MY INTENT (with a "T" NOT Intend) that brings your prayers into the NOW, in this incarnation, at this very moment in time. YOU MUST BE SPECIFIC!!!!!!!!!!!!!!

They live in "forever" time and in "all that is," so be VERY specific about exactly what you want and in the VERY SPECIFIC timeframe of what you want. Not being specific (intend) is never never land, or "which incarnation?" etc. to those on the other side.

I suggest that you say your prayer 3 times. 3 is the universal number.
* The first time sets your free will to ask for help,
* the second time your prayer creates intent
* the third time to me, means you"re really focused on getting this done!

Use the words Now, Forevermore and Always.
"Now," brings your prayer into the now, i.e. present. The Universe operates in a timeless forever and to have Them respond to your command you must state "now", otherwise your guides will be asking "in which incarnation, past life or parallel life do you want this done?"

"Forevermore," takes the prayer into all energy realms, incarnations and time frames.
Always," makes the prayer results continuous with no time lapses.

At the finale of your request Say: So be it, it is done. Thank you. "So be it," brings the prayer into the present life situation. "It is done," manifests that the prayer has become and IS a reality, NOW!

*** **Remember** if you change the wording of a prayer you will receive different results. You also need to take and make the appropriate actions in your life as follow through on your prayer request.

If you are asking for a confirmation, or to be shown something, ASK for a specific time and for a specific number of confirmations within that timeframe. I suggest 3 confirmation signs within 24, 48 or 78 hours.

Be sure to ask that these confirmations are shown to you in a manner that you as a human can understand as your confirmation. What"s obvious to God, you at this point, may not understand.

Prayer for Confirmation
Say: I ask and it is my intent to be able to see, recognize and understand any and all confirmation signs given to me by God/ The Universe. So be it, it is done.

If you do NOT get any confirmations, then KNOW that it may not be the time for you to have an answer. So try again and ask another way

When your prayers are answered, you have the support of a formidable crowd with the Universe and "all there is." If you feel that asking and praying for answers is too much, remember, there is a place in the Universe where your unasked questions are, the Gifts that you never requested and the guides you never used. Use all there is that is available to you and your soul's contract. ASK!

Armed with the knowledge of how to construct prayers for maximum results, the first thing to do every day, is to protect where your soul resides, your body.

Protecting/ Shielding
Think of it this way: your soul is a bright shining light like the light in a lighthouse. Your body surrounds and houses your soul, like the lighthouse encompasses its light. Your soul shines out of your eyes like the light shines out of the lighthouse.

Your soul is protected, because you are part of all that is. However, your body is <u>not</u> protected from the experiences of the earth school, like the lighthouse is not protected from the environment. Protect your soul"s house like the light keeper protects and maintains his lighthouse.

Your body can be shielded in a bubble/ cocoon of protective energy created through your intent. Think of the clear glass around a "snow ball." Its contents are protected no matter what is happening outside of that cocoon. As "Light keeper," within this bubble/ cocoon you are protected **if** you control life and direct your actions.

Asking and setting your intent to cocoon yourself in this protective bubble puts you in full control and charge of all that is available to you. When you are enclosed in your director"s room you are standing in full empowerment.

Being in that bubble YOU control your energy"s flow. YOU allow what affects you into your life. You can open the door and say "come on down" to bad energy and negative energies or entities.

Or you can selectively open yourself to people, events and environments that are for your highest and best good!

The cocoon concept saves an ENORMOUS amount of energy in defending yourself against detrimental energies or entities! You can use that extra energy to enjoy life or amp up your Gifts.

Prayer for all encompassing Protection:
Say: I ask and it is my intent, to surround myself in a seamless mirrored--(bubble or cocoon) of the Christ White Light (or whomever is your Higher Power), to protect me now, forevermore and always. Only allow the energy or entities which are for my soul's highest and best good to come thru. So be it, it is done. Thank you.

If you don't say anything else, this is what you need to say at any time in any place, whenever it's needed!

Why do I use the words seamless and mirrored? Seamless means nothing comes in or out unless you allow it. The concept of mirrored means that any negative energy or entity, event or whatever that is aimed at you, reflects back to the sender so that you will not be drained or affected. SO easy!

Who and what can be shielded?

Everything, anything and anyone! The protection bubble can be placed around you, your house, brother, pet, car, airplane, your travel"s path et al, hotel room and even another person (to use as they so choose to use so you do not interfere with their free will choice).

The reason you do not want to interfere with anyone or anything"s free will choice is because it"s THEIR Soul"s journey and THEIR soul"s choice of what to do with the energy you offer. Interfering with someone"s Karma will cause them to have to come back and redo everything in another incarnation.

If you have inadvertently or with intent tried to use your energy to influence or change the life of someone or something else, ask for forgiveness since it"s not YOUR job to handle their Karma. Then remove release and detach your energy from them immediately. At that time they will be free of your expectations and unaffected by your directives from that point forward.

For those asking how do I know that I will be forgiven, Trust that the Universe has answered your prayers.

If you need an extra boost of protection or a "quickie shield" use this method: with or without words visualize your sending palm facing outwards. Start at your root charka or lowest pubic area and make a rainbow arc that goes up to and over your head while, setting your intent and saying "shield, shield, shield." I use this when greeting negative people or while standing in front of the microwave heating my tea.

I suggest that you always maintain an awareness of how your energy field integrates with everything around you. If you feel "off," tired, cold, or an unspecified thing is bothering you, you have allowed an energy or entity to affect your control room!

Shield immediately then clean them out.

You are always in control of choosing the awareness level which creates or depletes your energy and empowerment.

Being slack on protection and cleansing will create an energy drain which will make you tired. Being slack will allow your energy to be siphoned and will impair your ability to be a conduit.

I surround myself every morning and extra shielding while I"m around hospitals, draining environments and people.

"Why do you spend so much time with shielding?"

The answer is twofold. First, it takes less time than brushing your teeth. (You can say it while brushing your teeth.) Secondly, you insure full empowerment of your Gift at all times.

It"s your choice how often you take care of or neglect protecting your "all you can be!" Clients ask why they have "burned out," "stay tired all the time" or aren"t "progressing and moving forward."

The first thing I ask is "do you shield and protect your Gift? They usually say, "My soul is protected, so why bother." I respond, its 2 separate issues.

If they are doing a protective ritual you can bet the verbiage is for short term or no coverage and non specific. How can their guides respond? Then I ask them, "Do you protect the body your soul resides in?" They say "why?" or "I do a little protection thing" or "oh I don"t do that."

The difference between long term extraordinary and ordinary is the way you protect your Gift and maintain your housing!

NO energy or entity can ever affect you unless you allow it.
You might want to paste that on your refrigerator! Memorize it in your being.

Shielding During Emergency Situations:

Emergency situations always present chaotic energy. Add an extra layer of shielding while working under that form of duress. To be safe while activating your healing energy as quickly as possible

Use the generalized prayer first, and then this work specific prayer.

Shielding Prayer for work:
Say: I ask and it is my intent to surround me, shield me, fill me and ground me with the Christ White Light (or whomever) to do your work now. Use me, use me, use me.

This is a short term prayer for a specific work situation.

This will immediately connect you to your guidance and activate your energy when there is no time for meditation or warm up techniques.

Medical and healthcare facilities and anyplace retain all the energy that ever was in, on and around their grounds and buildings. Remember that!

Shield yourself before you enter any healthcare facility or questionable environment. Clear the room you are working in (everything and every person that is in your life). Fill it with positive and physically healing and loving energy. As a healer, you can cover the room, hospital and client in a protective bubble if your client is going to remain in that location.

You can shield an operating room to control the energy of that area including each physician, nurse and staff. You must state that the bubbles" protection is to be used "as they so choose and only for their highest and best good." In that manner you are not interfering with Karma.

All rooms hold all of the energy and entities that were ever in that room as does the furniture, accessories, paint, wallpaper etc.

When leaving a healthcare facility or any environment or person that was taxing, I suggest clearing, releasing and detaching any and all energies and entities from your energy field as you walk to your next destination.

"Energy vampires" exist. Dark is always there because it balances Light. Both have to cohabit for the other to exist. Everything is energy. If you don't shield, anything that needs energy will try to siphon your life force energy.

I call dark energy "Moths" because they are attracted to light. As an example: when you turn on your back porch light at night, think of how many moths come to that light. When you go to a stadium game, think about the thousands of moths attracted to the greater wattage lights. Whew!

"Moths" create balance. The greater your Light, the more "moths" for balance. For those of you who have experienced entity and energy "blobs" at night, protect yourself by

1. Asking who they are (it''s a Universal law that they must answer)

2. Ask who they serve.

3. Then command them away by saying:

Prayer to Clean Your Personal Space:
Say: I ask, it is my intent and I command any and all energies or entities that are not for my highest and best good to leave my space now forevermore and always. So be it, it is done

The Universe is regulated so that all energies and entities (living or deceased) are required to respond to your free will choices for your space. To remove anything that you do not want in or occupying your space use the prayer above. I suggest 3 times!

FYI

An easy way to have continuous protection that has been used since time began is a sterling silver cross. History confirms, Monks wore a cross at their groin (root chakra) and nuns wore them over their heart area. Sterling silver repels negative energy. It removes all things negative, but MUST have a plain clean undecorated surface on the silver so any negative energy can be mirrored back to the sender.

General Shielding prayer:

Say: I ask and it is my intent to surround myself in a seamless mirrored cocoon of the Christ While light to protect me from any and all energies and entities in all of time, now forevermore and always. So be it, it is done, Thank you.

If at any point you doubt that you are not protected, use the prayer again. Doubting negates your original protection. Doing this on a daily basis is more vigilant that saying" well I said it once and I trust that I am always protected."

If you think you are always protected after only saying one prayer, you are incorrect because you interface with different energy situations within every environmental and people on an ongoing basis.

Cleansing Your Body & Surroundings

Your body bumps into the energies of EVERYTHING and entities as you move throughout life like those waves and salt spray in the Lighthouse scenario.

Every person that you have interfaced with in your life has created an impression and maintains an ongoing connection in your energy field unless you remove them. Every client you have come into contact with is plugged into your energy field until you release and detach from them.

Think about that. If you are a conduit and your pipeline is overlaid with multiple veils of energy and entities, then you are being drained by a gazillion active connections! And you wonder why you are tired and channel less energy?   Imagine your conduit ability IF you were like a clean PVC pipe with water flowing freely through it.

Is your pipeline one that has hundreds of screens over the initial portal with sludge throughout the pipe, mold on the walls and septic residue at the end? When you want to channel energy to a client, do you wonder why your energy is "not as effective or strong as it used to be?"

Clean your bubble shield every night, perhaps while cleaning your teeth or just before you fall asleep. It"s like cleaning a windshield of the car that has bugs embedded in the windshield grime that accumulated throughout your day.

The most effective routine, I find, to maintain the highest quality and quantity of ongoing energy and channeling excellence is to shield every morning and detach, remove and release energy and entities each night. Practicing this will give you more energy.

If you"re lazy with this maintenance routine, just remember, the brighter Light you are, the more "moths" you attract that can erode "all you are and can be" and you'll be covered in client sludge.

The following prayer will empower YOU to remove your own energy vampires.

Prayer to clean your energy field:
Say: I ask and it is my intent to remove, release and detach any and all energies and entities from my energy field that are not for my highest and best good, now forevermore and always. So be it, it is done.

Your energy field bubble needs to be cleaned just from "living your life" debris. Make an appointment with yourself to clean your energy field on a regular basis **at least** once a month.

Another method to clean your physical energy field.

Put 1/4 cup of sea salt or Epsom salt, (unless you have known sensitivities to either) in your bath water and stay in that water for ONLY 15 minutes. Staying in the water longer will deplete your energy. This helps remove toxins from your energy field.

If this is not possible, just take a short shower and let the water cleanse your field or you can hand spray yourself (like a Windex bottle) with salt water while showering.

Set your intent and state to yourself that the water is removing, releasing and detaching any and all energy and entities that are not for your highest and best good, now forevermore and always.

Advice for energy workers:

1. Remove, release and detach your clients on an appointment by appointment daily basis. You can do this by running water over your wrists for a few minutes between client sessions.

2. Remove daily debris with your cleansing prayer

3. Physically clean your full energy field at least once a month.

Prayer to remove energy from your energy field or your house, furniture, land, property etc.

Say: I ask and it is my intent to remove, release and detach any and all excess, unnecessary, preexisting, toxic or unhealthy energy or entities from _____ now forevermore and always. I ask that energy be replaced with the healing, loving energy of the Christ white light (or whomever is your power source), now, forevermore and always. So be it, it is done. Thank you.

Allowing Yourself to be Ready to Work

You've accepted your Gift and now have a client. That's when the self doubt sets in. Set your intent to "Use me" and ask to allow the energy of your Gift whatever that may be, to flow thru you.

God wants you to work and communicate in the manner that resonates with your free will choice under His guidance. Your training and Gifts are designed for the exact clientele that you are sent.

There is no competition.
No work is insignificant.

You are the **only** one who can diminish your Gifts or spiritual purpose with your belief system. IF you doubt, you impede the Universal flow thru you and your work. Ask to fine tune your Gifts. If you like your direction and it feels correct, go forward on that course. The Universe will redirect you by providing free will choice "nudgies," if you are not on track.

My specialty is MIDI and distant electromagnetic energy healing. When I started working with nerve regeneration and restoration I loved it! Stopping seizures half a world away was humbling and gratifying. Then I moved on to channeling the energy which reversed paralysis. That was incredibly awesome to look into a client"s face filled with disbelief and see them very childlike and gleefully practice the once lost function that was now restored.

My first client, a mother of 2 teenage boys, was told she would never walk again due to progression from MS to Devic''s Disease. After about 20 minutes, she could move her legs. I will never forget the look on her face.

I went home and stared at my hands for several days, afraid to touch anything. That''s when I knew it was NOT me and my Gift''s work was serious!

To this day, I feel privileged and blessed to be a conduit. However I can't fix bladder infections (unless it''s an electromagnetic stimulation issue.) Everything has its place and the "order of go" in which the Universe wants your Gift to benefit others. Your spiritual path is charted by your agreement with God/ the Universe while your free will determines the learning opportunities along the way!

Later on my path I received more and more clients that wanted a medical intuitive body scan. When I looked into bodies, after getting over the graphic visuals, I knew I had found my calling. I can see every organ, cell, nerve, tissue etc. I was humbled by it, I loved it and I love it!!!!!

You'll **know** when you have arrived where you belong. It's possible you'll be led into another direction as I was to write this book to help awaken your Gifts and further your life's purpose.

I never thought I would be doing this, until I realized that in college I minored in Writing! No coincidence there, the Universe was training me years ago!

Always know that when you allow the Universe to work through you, if you heal, influence or affect only one person in your life for their highest and best good, you have done a great job and fulfilled your spiritual purpose.

It's not necessary to completely stop what you are currently doing, just because you feel you have a calling for your Gift. You can maintain your current career and contribute to friends, colleagues and strangers.
Consider that you may have come to earth for both callings. You can also be highly Gifted and use it only once. Your agreement with the Universe determines your course in this incarnation.

This book is about accepting, trusting and living your spiritual purpose. Gifts come in all flavors: laughter, hiring people, art, philanthropic interests, saving the earth or animals and providing a simple pat on the back "atta boy/girl" to someone who needed your comment at that precise moment in time!

Allow what you and the Universe have agreed upon and don't ever feel "less than"!

Show up with
accountability,
responsibility,
and
integrity.

The Place between Allowing & Working

There is a place for a split second or longer when you have made all the right choices, have chosen to Trust, yet human self doubt **about what you can and can't do** eases its way into your mind. Even after you've crossed all your business T's and done your professional "stuff."

"I'm not sure what I am doing."

YES YOU ARE!

Your human ego "thinks you don't know what you are doing". YOUR SOUL KNOWS <u>exactly</u> what you are doing! Ask for Guidance.

Ego, self doubt and expectations create governors that diminish the "flow" of you Gifts.

It's NOT your job to know "how to do it."
God/ the Universe/ Your Higher Power know how to flow the energy and provide the information and instructions to get your spiritual job done in the exact manner with the EXACT appropriate outcome.

How do I determine if the "voices in my head" or my spiritual guidance are not ego? Any form of training that you are drawn to may activate your Gifts, your inner knowing and intuition. Your inner guidance will always lead you. Always listen to your heart and what resonates in your soul.

Spiritual guidance is a definite and different tone delivered in a soft yet firm directive manner. To insure that you are listening to your guidance

Prayer to Hear Your Guidance:
Say: I ask and it is my intent to set aside my ego and open my heart in Trust so I hear my guidance with complete unfiltered clarity. Now, forevermore and always. So be it, it is done!

Ask who the voice(s) work for; the Light, the dark? Or ask where your information is coming from. **Guidance is required to answer.**

If you have not shielded yourself and prepared correctly to allow the information to flow through you, you become a portal for dark energies and entities that have a freeway to come into the earth plane through you without reservation or boundaries and to communicate as they choose. NOT good! I say a VERY specific prayer before every session to take care of this issue.

Oftentimes while you are allowing the flow of the Gift through you, you will know you are doing everything correctly and communicating appropriately by confirmations from the Universe.

Chills, tingles, hair rising on your neck or other reoccurring signals that are individually yours mean confirmation from the Universe. This signals that what you are hearing or experiencing from Them or the client or the situation is "right on" solid Truth! Some people call goose bumps "God" bumps☺.

You also need to be aware of the downside of sensitivity. The downside of extra ordinary sensitivity is that you have a heart and a body that is empathetic and sympathetic, which makes you vulnerable.

Your "sensitivity" is what facilitates and substantiates your Gifts. Shielding yourself will prevent you from taking on anyone else's energy or problems and will maintain your ability to read while being empathetic towards the energy that you are reading.

The most important part is that shielding will keep their energy mess out of your energy field. Remember you have to be detached from any expectation and uninvolved in their "stuff" to be a pure conduit.

Many energy workers say, "I'm so tired after I've worked all day." Obviously they do not know how to shield themselves and orchestrate their energy correctly. Many intuitives and Light workers like the "drama" of being affected by their work and being humanly depleted by their "powers" or their quintessential sensitivity.

These individuals do not manage their Gift correctly and are degrading themselves and the professions by those statements. It's not a badge of honor to be possessed by your Gift!

The energy you spend on drama or being "affected" could be spent on facilitating helping someone.

Drama is a waste of energy. You don't get "points" for being so sensitive you are "affected", you only get "points" for doing work to benefit others.

Sometimes your sensitive sonar system, which is how you "feel" energy"s vibrational frequency, creates panic attacks, heart palpitations etc. because your energy system"s sensitivity is overloaded and unshielded. Shield!

If you are going through a Spiritual Awakening and experiencing some of the above symptoms, an online search will provide specific lists for the physical signs of an "awakening." Shielding during this time will smooth out or remove any unnecessary physical responses.

Below are fun exercises to practice maneuvering your energy field"s sonar system.

*Set your intent to pull your energy field in so you are indiscernible and have a friend try to locate you.

*Set your intent to "beam up" or locate a consenting friend.

These little practice tools teach you to "find" energy fields, which is how you learn to feel your client"s vibrational frequency no matter where they are located.

You can do this with your pets. Intuitives who locate lost individuals and pets or even corpses are pros at this technique!

What Can Affect Receiving a Client's Energy Information?

It is scientifically documented that energy is as strong and available when read remotely as it is "on site." This is possible **only if** the intuitive can access that frequency range. Actually the reader can focus more quickly because they"re not distracted by the client"s personal details and surroundings. However some things do affect receiving your client"s energy information.

Personal Blockages:

Did you know that RUBBER STOPS THE FLOW OF ENERGY? Think about it. What is around every electrical cord? Rubber! What kind of suits do the men who work on electrical lines wear? Rubber!

Energy flows up from the earth through one"s chakras and out through the crown.

Then it loops back down from the Universe in a figure 8 pattern. Right handed folks receive their earth energy coming up through their left side and send energy out through their right side. Left handed people are just the opposite.

Do you wonder why your wattage or reception is decreased and not as effective? If you wear heavy tennis shoes it's like putting your finger in an aquarium's intake filter. Those rubber shoes block the flow of everything that is supposed to be filtered in or out of your energy field.

Take off those rubber soled shoes shoes and you'll see a world of difference in energy and information flow!!

I recommend wearing leather, wood or cork bottomed shoes, preferably LEATHER! Yes, you can afford them. Go to the big fancy store, find your size and fit, then buy them online or at a discount shoe store.

Did you know that rubber soled shoes can keep you from sleeping? They create prickly feet, restless legs, leg cramps and lower back pain. Why, because your energy backs up and is creating your own energy septic tank. Soaking your feet in water will pull the "gunk" energy out out out.

Wearing socks or being barefooted will allow optimum energy flow. Your client''s information will be downloaded more rapidly due to no obstructions. These are ways to eliminate the causes for. "lower wattage," or "it makes me tired."

If you are still tired after work, also assess your methods of shielding, detachment and delivery procedures. Are you are using your own life force energy incorrectly or not protecting yourself?

Being an empath and personally experiencing a client''s sensations, diminishes the accuracy of your reading and information gathering. This is due to the fact that you are distracted and preoccupied by dealing with their sensations within YOUR body. Therefore you are not focused 100% on the client''s issues.

Additionally the empath experience lowers your personal "frequency" by energetically dealing with their issues within yourself! This also lowers the healing energy available to you because you are wasting personal energy processing their "stuff" **through** your body. Instead, examine the sensations on the monitoring mechanisms of your mind''s eye.

This way you are watching and registering what is going on and are not affected by what"s happening.

If you become empathically affected in the middle of a reading, then mentally use the remove, release detach prayer, and reshield. It is not a badge of honor to be an empath for your client because then you"re giving them less than 100%. Learn how to shield and use your energy!

Exterior energies around your client also alter their energy and affect your evaluation. Examples: Another healer"s energy will look like a green or red jellyfish in your client"s field. Radiation treatment creates a cap of red energy. If a client"s medication is too strong, it will produce a brown muddy sludge or just total darkness by numbing out the electromagnetics of the area controlled by the medication. Usually its pain meds that affect the energy read the most. That"s why I ask the client to shower or bath before our session if possible.

Be sure a client gives you permission to enter their energy field and is not just placating this reading because someone wanted them to have this done! A "half" permission from a client creates a half baked assessment.

Personal Preparation

I schedule intensive intuitive energy tasks first thing in the morning after my shower or after lunch so I can take time to get quiet in order to be extremely focused on each client"s issues.

For emergency healing energy or body scans, take a quick walk, sit or stand in a quiet space for about 1 minute while taking a few deep breaths. Then ask permissions and say your prayers. In a few minutes you'll be ready. Use me Use me Use me!

Preparation for a regular appointment:

1. Take a few minutes of quiet time, get yourself balanced, centered and grounded.

2. Take off your shoes for better "connection." You can stand on a towel if you're in an area with inappropriate floors. Example: Hospital rooms, veterinarians, examining areas, etc.

3. Protect and shield yourself with prayer. This works for intuitives, life coaches, and spiritual consultants as well.

4. Have a glass of water or two handy and drink it during your reading or consultation.

If you need to take a "loo" break during the reading, fill up that glass and have some more water with a few lemon drops in it to keep the headaches away.

5. Move away from computers, clocks, cell phones, iPods etc.

Be sure to shield yourself from any outside electromagnetic activity that could affect your focus (see 5 above as some examples). Hospital, healthcare facilities and ICU are different, always double shield yourself and go to work!

You as Your Client

To perform a healing energy session, body scan or MIDI on yourself, ask to see your body"s energy field. Employ the same systematic approach you use for a client you may experience "raw" eyes and a frontal 3rd eye headache.

Drinking lemon juice in water or ½ cup of Gatorade or V8 will help relieve those symptoms. Magnesium in chocolate will also help. Channeling depletes magnesium, that"s why a lot of spiritual individuals crave chocolate.

Do not have to leave your body to do this. Set your intent to view your body as if it were your client.

Client Preparation before a Reading

First, explain to your client how you conduct your session or reading.

Initial connection with the client's energy

Before starting any spiritual, healing, intuitive session or life purpose consultation, have an informal chat session with the client about all sorts of things (fun, serious and non-directed) to get a "feel" for their energy.

Talk about their work, the family and all things except the work you"re preparing to do.

If you sense the client thinks the chatter is non productive, inform them that you are using this to identify their energy so it will be more readable.

Before each consultation

1. Ask client''s permission!

2. Say preparation prayer to protect the client and you.

Preparation Prayer:
Changing the words will change the results.

Say: Thank you God/ Universe/ Higher Power for the Gift of _____. I ask and it is my intent to surround me, shield me, fill me and ground me with the Christ White Light (or your Higher Power.) I ask that all those energies, entities, angels and all those on the other side who're in charge of my soul''s contract that serve the Christ White Light (or your Higher Power) contribute to this consultation now and all those in charge of_____''s contract come and work through me now only for _____''s highest and best good. I ask that _____ and I have no expectations for this session and have no human filters so that THY will be done and that the information and energy will be pure and not tainted. I ask that You use me, use me, use me, ONLY for _____''s highest and best good. Thank you. SO be it, it is done!

Having no expectations or filters (attitudes) allows your Higher Power to do what"s best. Human expectations alter the information"s purity. The difference between being an ordinary healer and extraordinary one is the ability to be a pure conduit.

By "not caring enough" or not having any expectations, you are channeling pure information. When you"re creating situations with your expectations and your human filters, YOU are limiting and tainting the Universe"s "all there is."

Don"t get so caught up in over thinking, techniques and ego that you forget to be a pure channel.

The Universe determines everything.

Asking permission to enter your client's energy field is the most important aspect of any session.

If you proceed to read clients that haven"t given you permission to work with them, you are not connecting to pure information. I inform my clients that every energy worker, spiritual counselor, intuitive, psychic, etc. they encounter should ask them for permission because it is not always implied just by making an appointment.

Remind the client to have each practitioner detach from their energy for their safety and explain that you will detach from their energy field when finished with your assessment.

Now it's time to show up and go to work!

Trust the

information given

to you

by your Guides

and Higher Power

How to Convey Information You Receive

Some practitioners tell clients information on an "as needed basis." I do not agree with this concept. It doesn"t honor the Gift of direct information your client receives through you.

I believe that good, bad or ugly, each client has the right to the information provided and that it"s the client"s right and Karma to choose WHAT to do with that knowledge.

If you"re asked a question of if there is a gap in your information that you do not know, have a clue, or aren"t sure, TELL the client exactly that! Then ask them if you can email or call them back later after you "think about this for a while."

I had a client from Asia that was being misdiagnosed. Our reading was a very long precise and accurate one. We decided that she should go to the Mayo clinic for treatment.

Throughout the entire process she would call me about once a week and ask me if I was hearing "Cancer." I NEVER got the word "Cancer." I got that she was going to be fine. I told her that if I had heard the word Cancer, I would have relayed that information to her.

Again and again she called all hours of the day and night wanting to know if it was Cancer. Each time I assured her that I never got the word Cancer and if I did, I would tell her. I understood! If it was me, I would want to know.

After she was thoroughly re-diagnosed at Mayo, all the information that I was given about the interior physical deterioration, surgery description, post operative outcome and future prognosis and probabilities were 100 % correct and "right on" in location and size. The client then informed me "it was Cancer!"

I was furious and felt betrayed by my Guides. I had always completely believed in what they said! I decided that if I was going to get erroneous information, I would quit this profession. I only wanted the truth.

I stopped consultations. A few months later the client called and asked again if I ever heard the word Cancer and had I held it back to not frighten her. I told her no and that I was no longer doing consultations because HER information was given to me incorrectly. Even though every other detail, except the word Cancer, was 100% accurate including that she is now completely fine!

I asked her feelings on my not conveying the ONE thing she feared most. She quietly said "I need to tell you something and you need to go back to work. If you had told me it was Cancer before I left, I would have considered something different and never have gone to Mayo. However since you did say everything was going to be OK, I decided to be treated. Thanks to you I am now Cancer free and in remission."

The lesson is: When the Universe/ God knows that a client can"t handle specific information, the Universe will NOT give that information to YOU. Trust the Universe!

I came out of that experience with an even stronger belief that the information that I am given is for the highest and best good of my client at all times! No matter what my little earthling mind thinks it knows!

SO now I trust even more!!!

The responsibility for clear accurate information is determined by the Universe and NOT by your guessing or interpretation.

All intuitive information is provided from the Universal library, resources and omnipotence.

Trust that information in the face of all the facts that might approximate another conclusion. Then you stand in truth. Always listen to what resonates within you.

I do not censor, reformulate or give information on an "as needed basis." I feel this practice reinforces the integrity and authenticity of the Gift channeling through me.

Detach, remove
and release from
your client

Go onto your next
experience
unaffected by
energy, issues or
entities

"Learning Opportunities"

"Don't touch her, she could give you energy."

A lady had seen me work with her best friend who had come to me with 4th stage breast cancer. After our work together her friend is in remission.

While in the garden department of Wal-Mart, buying my spring flowers, I saw her. She introduced me to her husband. As I reached over to shake his hand, she jerked him away saying "don"t touch her she could give you energy."

Lesson: Sometimes your Gift is perceived by others incorrectly. Hold fast to the good and how it benefits others.

Use your talents wisely

After being on holiday, while unpacking my travel cases I twisted, bent down and tried to lift my hanging bag. I later learned that in the medical community that movement is called torque.

As I fell on the floor I heard a crunch and couldn"t get up. I was delivered to the emergency room on a spinal board.

After x-rays the physician said they saw nothing. Having the Gifts that I do, I was able to look at myself and see the fracture! I mentioned to the doctor that I wanted an MRI and another x-ray. He complied with a MRI and suggested that I might have a slight fracture.

I found another facility with advanced equipment that MRIed me from the perspectives I requested. The images confirmed the fracture. My physicians prescribed the appropriate medications and treatments. I added my alternative therapies.

Lesson: When you know your Gift has provided accurate information, use and present it wisely to help navigate those who don"t have your expanded awareness. I believe that Integrative medicine is the best combination for every client!

Intuition by Permission only

While visiting a male friend"s family at their beach residence, I would see him in the distance stop and catch his breath. This was a robust and hearty fellow, so of course this symptom was never mentioned to me.

I on the other hand, intuitively picked up each incidence with trepidation. However I did NOT tap into his energy to see what was going on.

At sunset one evening on the front porch, I casually asked if I could look into his body. With a cocktail under his belt he bellowed "sure." I did a quick body scan and saw something that I needed to tell him. I decided to wait until the next morning after we all went for our bike ride.

I casually said, "Have you had your aortic valve checked recently?" He told me he had JUST gotten his yearly physical and was pronounced fine. I told him that his valve was bad and if he kept up his party lifestyle including fried foods etc. it would be a disaster in the making.

I asked him to "humor" me and ask his doctor to recheck his aortic valve when he returned two weeks later for his follow-up visit. Jim remarked that his physician did not find a problem with that valve during his initial visit and could not imagine how, with all the testing, it was missed. But he would "humor me" and do what I asked.

Returning from his appointment, he greeted me rather pale. He informed me there was a problem with his valve that had been missed in his annual checkup. At that point Jim asked if I saw anything else and was more receptive to my remarks and actually listened.

I told him that with his fried foods, "wine, women and song" lifestyle, he was going to have a heart attack and would need bypass surgery in 2 years. He said "I'm going to live and enjoy my life." I said "your choice."

Several years later (2 to be exact), out of the blue, I received an email from another friend. She said "I thought you might want to know that Jim had an unexpected quadruple bypass yesterday." I had forgotten my prognosis and told her I'd check on him.

I asked why he had not let me know. He replied "it was exactly one day shy of your 2 years prediction." He said he told only his Mother "because I didn't want to hear you tell me, I told you so!"

Lesson: Each person chooses their life path, no matter how much you would like to warn them or make it easier for them with your knowledge.

Bless their choices, make no judgments and keep on loving them the way they are.

Blessed and filled with joy

Remember when we addressed How old are you?? Let''s do it again. Declare that you are going to live to be 100. Now let''s determine what percentage of your life you''ve already "used up" 45%, 60 %?? This is a reality check. At 50 you''ve used up 50%. Ask yourself: how are you going to use your LIFE with the time you have left?

Although your spiritual purpose is fulfilling and you''re leading a blessed life, sometimes you may feel something is missing and that you are empty. It''s a subject no one ever talks about.

Working "in service" is God's work.
However, you also need to make time to nourish your human spirit and life. Make an appointment with YOURSELF to do something for or that feeds your soul! It''s the most important "work" and balancing element you can add to your well being.

No one but YOU can remember and make time to support you! If you don't honor you and your earth life, no one else will. Fill yourself up, so you can be a brighter light to help others. Practice what you preach! Tomorrow never comes! Do it today!

Every day **is** NEW. Try to wake up each morning with a childlike wonder of "what are we going to do today?" That perspective will make you more alert and add freshness to your life.

Freshness creates Joy!

In closing the only thing you have to worry about is **nothing**! The Universe will always catch and redirect you if you're off course.

Every morning before you get out of bed...

Prayer for start of each new day
Say: God, I ask and it is my intent that you send to me today all those that would benefit from my services and those that will benefit my life. Send them to me without delay. Stop any and all energy or entities that interfere with or impede my joy. So be it, it is done! Thank you, Amen.

THIS ONE REALLY WORKS!!!!!!!

Now, go home and enjoy your life on Earth!

Professionalism

Business before Your Session

Traditional medicine uses forms and contracts. If you are doing any form of healing, consultation or intuitive work, I suggest you use a legal release and client information forms for your practice. Even if you are an intuitive consultant for business, or a life coach, you might want to protect yourself from "expectations."

Did you know that you can be sued for creating false hope and expectations within another person's mind? If anything goes wrong, no matter what was said verbally, you're on the hook. Ask yourself, could any of the services I offer create any false expectations from an unreasonable person? If so, you need an agreement.

A client consent release form and master information sheet is part of a complete client file and encourages committed clients. Most of the professional world requires informational and release paperwork, why wouldn't you?

You are welcome to use my client forms as a template or any portions thereof at www.BrentEnergyWork.com and located at the end of this section

Attitude

There is no competition. The Universe sends you the exact clients for your special Gifts and spiritual purpose in perfect timing. If you need to persuade a client to work with you that's not a good sign. You have already tainted the purity of the energy and spiritual exchange.

Your job is to open the door or expand the view. The client or recipient must choose what to do with the information that you provide.

Value Your Gift

Your Gift or spiritual purpose's contribution is just that. Do not devalue your ability for fear of losing business or dismiss your contribution for the lack finances or emotional and spiritual support. God/ the Universe determine the value.

Certification of Your Gift!

Should I have certification and degrees from all the masters, teachers and universities? That"s your choice! I am certified by God and client results!

You may have umpteen educational doctorates, multiple lettered degrees and several titles. NO one"s work is more important than anothers. We use our contributions in different area assignments with unique qualifications for this incarnation"s mission.

In the middle of the night I received a frantic call from a friend desperate for help for her best girlfriend who was admitted to the hospital on a ventilator due to fluid accumulation in her cancerous lungs. She wasn"t expected to live till morning.

I agreed to help. I did a MIDI and directed healing energy all night. By dawn she had stabilized and was being weaned from the ventilator. Her doctors were floored and had never thought results of this nature were possible.

Several days later when Best Friend was able to talk, she called and thanked me. She wanted me to meet and work with her doctor who was with Sloan Kettering.

At her insistence I spoke with her doctor on the phone and the conversation went like this:

D: "Tell me Ms Atwater, what IS it that you do?"

B: "I say my prayers, set my intent, focus, watt up and send healing energy to my client to facilitate the desired results."

D: "And where did you get your medical training?"

B: "I have none."

D: "Where did you study medicine?"

B: "I have never studied medicine."

D: "And where do you get your information"

B: "From the voices in my head."

D: "Lets" see, you have never studied medicine, have no medical training and get your information from „voices in your head", is that correct?"

B: "yes Sir"

D: "Who do you think you are, interfering in my patients" life and why do you even think you can help her?"

B: "Because of her results."

D: "You leave my patient alone!"

B: "No sir, She"s hired me to facilitate her healing!"

And so goes certification!!!

Training and Certification

Does having 24 certificates on the wall make you feel better or more secure? If it does, by all means go get several.

I think the various approaches, methods and theories of healing modalities and intuitive development training programs, universities and colleges are absolutely wonderful IF they ignite your soul"s remembrance of the Gift"s you"ve come to contribute.

However, never doubt that you, like I, might be in the "just do it" Club (as the Nike ad says). What matters most are the benefits and results your client receives, not framed degrees and certifications.

Professional Behavior

Many new practitioners will answer the phone any hour of the day or night, on any day of the week and then complain about their client base. Set parameters of what you want: Clientele, office hours, etc. Value what you do, so others will too.

If you don"t value your time, neither will anyone else. (They"ll always take a free sample.) Ask the Universe to bring you the type of client that you think you want. Then you can determine if it"s truly your direction. Sometimes a multitude of multi tiered directions are part of expanding your journey and not the specific end of your trip.

I incorporated my business under the suggestion of an attorney. In today''s world, as sad as it may be; there are individuals who will try to sue for no apparent reason when you have worked on them in good faith.

If you are incorporated, then your personal losses should be less, if the "business" is sued.

Professional Presentation

If you want to be treated as a professional you have to be one! Can you imagine Carolyn Myss or Dr. Oz saying "Love and Light" to a neurosurgeon after leaving intensive care? You get my point!

Have you ever heard the phrase "dress for success?" Or "you only have one chance to make that first impression?" Both are true.

Professional presence is a must! If you want to be considered part of the healthcare or business staff, you need to look like the expert practitioner that you are. Too casual no matter how its touted is not business appropriate and should be for everyone else. I suggest your presence provides a good visual resume so your client can point to you and say, oh, that''s MY practitioner and be proud of it!

IF you are on a tight budget, upscale consignment shops, Junior League shops, Goodwill and discount stores can provide economical business attire. Online clothing and shoe outlets and eBay, all offer affordable prices. You have no excuse not to dress for success!

Privacy

HIPAA privacy laws state that under no condition are you allowed to give client names, health or personal information or circumstances. Even to relate their "story," you must have their permission in writing. Your work with each client is confidential!

What do I charge for my services since "I don't think I know what I'm doing?"

Ask your guides. The Gift and your Spiritual Purpose will unfold through your vision. Do not discount your guidance; it is there for a reason. Your inner knowing will tell you what to charge all along the way. ASK!

You have EVERYTHING YOU EVER NEED, so JUST ASK!

I was "told" to start at $185.00, why those figures- I have no idea. I had lots of clients. Then I decided to lower my fees to "help" folks. I lost client volume. When I went back to work for $185.00, the Universe sent my client base back.

No fee schedule determines your greatness!

You will get the exact client and number of clients in the exact group that you came to serve! Think Mother Theresa. Oprah helps in healing others by expanding awareness. Healers, energy workers, spiritual counselors, masters, intuitive developers, life coaches, psychics etc. come in all forms and walks of life.

No one spiritual purpose is more important than the other. It"s just a specific assignment level in this incarnation. If your clients are falling off, then also reassess your fee scale. The Universe has a way of redirecting your course if you"re not on track. How can the Universe help you, if YOU stand in the way???

ASK!

Billing

It is my practice for a client to fill out a contract prior to our appointment. It insures that the client is serious. This contract includes a forfeiture clause should the client be unable to notify my office that they need to reschedule. I believe as a single practitioner, who conducts multiple hour consultations, that this establishes a solid foundation for your business and time.

Payment

If you give things away "free," i.e. the "receivee" just walks away and hopefully says thanks, then that transaction has a Karmic debt of "owing." It is unbalanced no matter how much "good" you think you did.

Many healers think "giving away with love" is "doing good." That thought is partially correct. Often the "giver" feels empty inside, depleted of resources and unfulfilled. One sided transactions are unbalanced and an open Karmic debt.

Feeling satisfied and pleased with your exchanges is the correct emotional response.. ANY interchange in life must have balanced giving AND receiving.

I require my clients to prepay for their appointment in order to secure a place in my schedule. Sadly, before I adopted that practice, I had many that "promised to pay" the other half at the end of the appointment or for a sliding fee on a monthly basis and never did. Now I accept their credit card. Its payments are their monthly remittance for our session.

Sliding Scale Fee

It"s your choice to present a sliding scale fee. I do not find it appropriate for my client base. Over the years I have found that when people ask for a discount, it later becomes apparent in other conversations that they have spent "thousands" with doctors and other professionals and practitioners.

You can"t imagine the stories that I"ve heard about why someone can"t pay. I politely inform them that while I appreciate their candor and understand a budget, when their financial situation changes we"ll make an appointment.

My heart chooses the recipients of my pro bono work in hospitals, with veterinarians, rescue leagues and just plain folks.

Discounts and "Specials"

I've seen many practitioners give "free" sessions in order to lure business. Almost everyone will take a free sample of almost anything. Renowned educators, lawyers, entrepreneurs or physicians do not have to give free lectures, consultations or surgeries. Your reputation for accuracy, knowledge, integrity and client results will bring business to you.

Advertising "freebies" looks like you need to attract clients for your work. I prefer to stand in knowledge and Trust that I get exactly who I'm supposed to work with and when, rather than "hawk my wares."

Many practitioners also give volume or bulk discount rates. Have you ever heard of a hospital MRI, x ray or CT scan technician say "since we have viewed this area in your body on multiple occasions, we are going to give you a discount"? Or lawyers say, "We've addressed this issue multiple times, you've earned a discount."

Have you ever heard a person going into the emergency room or asking their dentist, "Will you perform your services for less?" **after** they have scheduled the appointment?

To me, if you have a new or strong practice, you are undermining your work by giving discounts. Potential clients will wait until you are having a "special," or ongoing customers will continually be asking for a "discount."

Do you think Carolyn Myss, Louise Hayes, Judith Orloff, Dr. Northrup, Deepak Chopra, Dr. Oz or whomever you admire make a practice of giving discounts?

Even *"The Secret"* crowd would just set their intent and manifest business.

Do pro bono work yes, charitable contributions yes, educational materials yes, donate presentations at learning centers yes. If in doubt ask yourself, how would your favorite professional handle this?

Although hard times may necessitate the financial question, in my opinion, it"s disrespectful to the holistic and integrative medicine community. If it"s necessary, clients should ask if you will lower your fees for their situation **before** a session and not prey on your "love" based profession.

I also understand helping those under financial duress, we"ve all been there.

However, because it"s a "Gift" or Spiritual Path and "you work from Love" doesn"t pay the bills.

Frustrated and strapped "healers," spiritual gurus, life path professionals and intuitive developers filled with "joy" AND underlying stress, need to rethink and revaluate their business practices. Even ministers are paid salaries by the Church as are the Pope, the Rabbis, etc...

Many professionals and practitioners will take whatever they can get during *any hour of the day or night* to try to "prove" their worth or "giving for love." No parameters create no respect!

In the allopathic world, you go to the physician that your budget and or insurance, network or circumstances necessitates and there is no "discussion" prior to your appointment regarding fees. You accept the billing of the healthcare provider that you have chosen, or you search for one that offers the services you need in your price range. In business you shop where you can afford to do so, or you "save up" for something special!

Bartering

Many integrative, holistic, alternative therapists and spiritual professionals barter with each other by exchanging services. This appears to be a common practice. I do not feel that this promotes professionalism. When I have been to conferences as a keynote speaker, many individuals come up to me and ask "would you just take a quick look at me?"

I tell them to contact me after the event is over. When they call my office I have them fill out the forms and make payment just like a client, which they requested to be. This may sound harsh and it makes some folks a bit miffed, however during the same time I would be doing a "Freebie," I could be helping an individual resolve their health issues. With every rule there is an exception. Let your heart tell you what to do.

Most traditional medical personnel or individuals in the same professions do offer a percentage off "to professional equals and their immediate family." I feel this trade practice acknowledges real world finances AND professional respect.

I also receive an extraordinary amount of email from practitioners asking me how to work with their energy, do a treatment for their client and a range of assorted questions about their personal energy, spiritual work, and intuitive practice.

DO "e mailers" ever think about the time it takes to write a detailed answer to their question? In a way it"s flattering that they value your opinion, however it"s also disrespectful of your professional life and personal time!

The examples I mention above are based on professional healthcare, private business standards and the necessity of maintaining a balanced life.

Just because you work for God / the Universe and God is love, you don"t have to give your Gift away in order to prove your worth and validate your spiritual servitude. Then complain to your friends, family and business colleagues, that you can"t make a living and pay all the bills. There will be many opportunities to give your Gift from your heart.

If this sounds like you, you might want to rethink your business practices.

Charitable Donations

If you want to make charitable donations in a professional manner, set aside a special timeframe or day for pro bono work. Inform your clients or advertise that day as your "give back" day. Then keep a list of the clients, the services you provided, with a dollar amount affixed to each service and give that to your accountant at the end of the year as your charitable contributions.

Join an all volunteer health organization like Volunteers in Medicine or donate your time and talents to local community outreach, career, educational, trade school or business facilities.

Emergency Paperwork

The emergency room requires that you or someone with you fills out paperwork for the triage nurse and hospital records. I suggest your office require those forms also.

Emergency situations should not eliminate paperwork! Those promising to "call back or come back and give you their information," sadly, are not always reliable. It took my heart about 10+ years to learn that!

Death

If your client dies, you do not owe a refund. The hospital, doctors and veterinarians that treated the patient will send charges, as will the funeral home, lawyers and all other businesses that were involved up to the time of death. It is my suggestion that as a professional, do not dismiss your charges by "being nice" unless your heart tells you otherwise. Death is part of the circle of life.

In Summary

I spend a lot of time working for free in veterinarian clinics, nursing homes, hospitals and private consultations. Often I"ll extend my services and hours way beyond what the client has purchased to help them get on tract. I don"t advertise it. My heart and guidance tells me who and how to help, let yours do the same.

Websites & Fees

If you have a website, I believe that you should publish your rates. A lot of practitioners do not publish their fees. It"s ethical to state your charges up front.

Website Disclaimers

The following is a standard Disclaimer and should be in all bold.

THIS WEBSITE IS FOR INFORMATIONAL AND ENTERTAINMENT PURPOSES ONLY AND IS NOT A SUBSTITUTE FOR (FILL IN THE BLANK FOR YOUR CATEGORY).

For Healers, other medical disclaimers should also need to be displayed.

For any spiritual practitioner, I suggest that you display an appropriate disclaimer which can be prominently seen.

Business Forms

The Client Release and Contract should contain the following: (add specifics for your practice.)

Client Release and Contract on date
Please fill required spaces marked with the red X between Your Name and
_____ ("Client") of

Please print Name
X _____Full
Address

I understand that Your Name of your business is an type of business and does not present herself as a medical doctor nor as possessing any formal medical training, nor as a licensed, registered or certified practitioner or counselor. (Leave out some verbiage if you are certified)

In consideration of the promises and conditions contained herein, I seek and it is my intent to hire Your Name for what you do. As further consideration for Your Name's Services, I agree to provide certain current, complete and accurate information about myself as required on Your Name's client information form. No one representing your business or Your Name offers me any false hope, false promises, expectations, warranties, or assurances of the success or the outcome of any of Your Name's work

I have read and understand Your Name fees and that they are pre paid BEFORE my appointment is scheduled and non refundable. I agree to the payment conditions and to pay the total fee amounts for Your Name's services in US Funds.

I choose the following service (s). Please write clearly
1. _____ Fee: _____ X

2. _____ Fee: _____

Additional Fees if applicable: Emergency: _____ Travel: _____

Initial Total fees are: _____ X

If I pay by debit or credit card, I understand that by providing the following information to <u>YOUR NAME</u> and <u>YOUR COMPANY</u>

that I agree to and I legally authorize that the debit or credit card below be charged to pay for <u>Your Name"s</u> Consultation(s).

If I pay via PayPal, I agree to and authorized that transaction to pay for <u>YOUR NAME</u> services.

The PayPal email address is <u>YOUR EMAIL ADDRESS</u>

I understand and agree to the following:
a. if I need to reschedule my appointment, that I am required to give _____ "s office 24 hour notice.

b. If I miss my appointment, without giving <u>Your Name"s</u> office a 24 hour notice for rescheduling, I will be charged the full fee for <u>your business activities</u> and_or Travel arrangements.

c. I phone <u>Your Name</u> for my sessions and pay the charges.

I am eighteen (18) years of age or older, of sound mind and not under any mind altering drugs. By signing this agreement, I acknowledge that I have read the above, have thoroughly reviewed and understand its contents and that I am giving my informed consent and it is my intent to agree to this contract. By my written acceptance of this agreement, I know this document becomes a legally binding contract and is confidential. This Contract shall be governed by and construed in accordance with the laws of the State of <u>YOUR STATE</u>.

X <u>Signature: </u> Seal

Date: _____

X Witness: _____

<u>Consent by Legal guardian, Parent or Attorney in Fact</u>.

As the Parent and or Legal Guardian, or POA, I acknowledge that I have read the above, have thoroughly reviewed and understand its contents and that I am giving my informed consent. It is my intent to agree to this contract.

I authorize you to provide services for:
_____ (Client).

X Signature:_____ Seal

Date: _____

X Witness: _____

Your Company Logo and Name
Address
Town, State, Zip code
Office Phone: Fax: Email

Client Release and Contract on   date

Page: 2 of 2

Be sure to fill in the required spaces marked
with the red X

My payment method for my appointment(s)
is: Please check one of the following
Personal Check: _____ Money Order: ___
Pay Pal: ____Credit or Debit Card: _____
Type of card: _____

X Name as it appears on the card: _ _

X Card number, Please Print CLEARLY: _

X Expiration date of card _____

X The last three numbers on signature strip:

<u>The Billing Name and Address as it appears on the card's statements:</u>

X_____

X _____

X _____

X _____

You will receive instructions for your appointment(s) when it is scheduled.

Thank you.

Disclaimer: (for those working in healthcare)

Disclaimer: YOUR NAME is not a medical doctor nor associated with any branch of allopathic medicine. YOUR NAME is a DESCRIPTION OF YOUR WORK. YOUR NAME DESCRIPTION OF YOUR WORK opinions are based on HIS/HER intuition and should not be a substitute for a medical examination and are not a substitute for medical procedures or treatments. ALWAYS consult a physician or trained health care professional concerning diagnosis for any medical problem or condition and before undertaking any diet, health related or lifestyle change programs. As in traditional medicine, there are no guarantees with YOUR WORK.

Client Information Form

Business name, address etc information as header

Client Information Form All client information is strictly confidential and secure. Please fill this out completely and Mail, Fax or email to address listed above. Thank you

CLIENT NAME: _____

PARENT'S NAME:

_____

CLIENT BIRTH DATE:
_____TIME:___PLACE:____

OCCUPATION: _____

Please include CLIENT PHOTO: _____

HOME ADDRESS:

_____

HOME PHONE: _____

EMAIL HM: _____

HOME PHONE 2:_____

CELL: _____

OFFICE PHONE: _____

EMAIL OFF: _____

Alternative contact: _____

Phone: _____

Referring Physician /Specialist/
Practitioners):

A good time to call to schedule your
appointment ____

IS Email communication easy for you?

_____

What are convenient times for your
appointment? _____

All appointments are made in (your time
zone): **Time-Zone Converter link for your
time zone appointments**

Your Name- Client Information Form p 2

What issues do you want addressed?

Who are your Medical / Holistic and
Integrative providers?

What Alternative treatments are you
currently working with?

What Medicines or Herbs are you currently
taking?

Additional Comments about things that you
would like me to know that you feel would
be helpful information.

Preparing Your Client for the Appointment

After the client has sent in their initial paperwork, I suggest you send out a time schedule and confirmation letter providing the time (stating your time zone) or times that you have or can be available for them and include instructions for their forthcoming appointment.

Confirmation Letter Below is a sample form. You are welcome to use any sections that are appropriate for your business.

■■■■■■■■■■■■■■■■■■■■■■■■■■■■■■■■■■■■

Business Heading
Full Address
Phone & Fax
Email

Thank you for choosing my work as part of your <u>healthcare and healing</u> journey. Your information has been received and your payment has secured your appointment.

Between receipt of your application and timing of your appointment getting scheduled on my calendar varies sometimes a few days, 2-3 weeks, or longer.

*** In order to guarantee your time slot, ASAP please confirm that you received your instructions and are able to comply with your appointment time.***

Although I appreciate and understand your enthusiasm in your <u>healing</u> journey, please do not call me to see when your appointment is scheduled. Please do not send multiple "nudgie" emails or call to see if I have received your emails.

I will address any questions that have arisen in our next session. All appointments are set at the appropriate time to facilitate your journey. If I need to change your appointment time I will notify you in ample time.

INITIAL INFORMATION:

1. Please don't forget to email or mail me your photo <u>BEFORE</u> our session. Do NOT fax your photograph.

2. You are required to give 24-hour notice to reschedule your appointment. Otherwise you will be charged your full fee.

BEFORE APPOINTMENTS:

BEFORE your appointment, please check your phone messages and email.

** If I am called for an emergency, I will do my best to notify you.

PHONE the number provided at your appointment's Eastern Standard Time, Convert your Eastern Standard Time appointment time to YOUR local time zone.

International clients may want to use their late night free cell phone hours, a prepaid card or other calling card for low rates.

DELAYS: Sometimes my schedule gets backed up. Please allow a 30-minute window around your appointment time. If the phone is busy at our appointed time, wait a few minutes and try again. Do not call my mobile phone to see why my office phone is busy. I will answer as soon as possible.

Since I have a lot of clients that may be on multiple medications or under duress and in medical situations that might affect their clarity, I provide Instructions form. You might want to make one for your clients.

CONSULTATION:

1. We will have a consultation to identify your health issues.

2. We will choose a mutually agreeable time and date for your energy work during our consultation

Prior to your **Energy work** Session

I ask that you take a bath. Put 1/4 cup of sea salt or Epsom salt, (unless you have known sensitivities to either) in your bath water and stay in that water for ONLY 15 minutes or your energy will be depleted. This helps cleanse your energy field. If this is not possible, just take a short shower and set your intent to let the water cleanse your field.

1. I prefer for you to be in a QUIET environment, without any distractions and that you not have anyone else near you during our session. You may have a pet in the room.

2. Please refrain from eating heavy or greasy food and drinking alcohol or smoking 24 hours before and after our session.

3. Please refrain from eating 1 hour before Energy Work.

4. I would also prefer that you have not had another energy treatment at least 3 days prior to our session as your body may still be adjusting to the recalibration of the another treatment or procedure. (Emergencies are an exception).

What to Expect:

You remain fully clothed, however I ask that you remove all watches and anything metal that you might be wearing. I prefer that you are barefooted.

Have your palms facing upwards and do not cross your hands or feet. Crossing your hands or feet disrupts the Energy flow and the release of toxic unhealthy energy.

For personal safety, if you are having on site energy healing done, I ask that you allow 30 minutes remaining stationery after your energy work before you drive, or that you have someone with you who can drive you to your destination.

After your Energy work:

I ask that you drink water with lemon juice in it for 3 days following our session, unless you are intolerant to lemons or their chemical content or have any other factors that would prohibit their use (meds, or a disorder).

This keeps your electrolytes balanced while your body is releasing, restoring & adjusting to your new frequencies. Thank you.

Message to Book Clubs and Professional Associations and Organizations

I'd be delighted to speak with you over the phone or in person.

*** Many individual have requested that I put all the prayers and affirmations in one place so they can access them quickly, so I created the book

Prayers to Empower Your Life's Spiritual Purpose

Other Just Plain Love® Titles
in Audio, eBooks, Hardcover, Kindle and Paperback

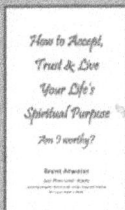

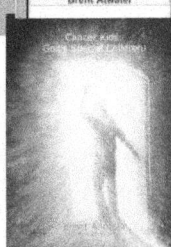

BOOKS
by
Brent Atwater

About Brent Atwater

At age 5 Brent"s intuitive talents were discovered by Duke University"s Dr. J B Rhine in his initial study for ESP.

Ms. Atwater has the extraordinary gift to see inside a body to accurately diagnose current and future issues.

Ms Atwater"s specialized medical intuitive diagnostic abilities have earned her the nickname of the "human MRI." Her practice has highly respected, evidence based, documented and published cases. In 1987 Brent founded the Just Plain Love® Charitable Trust.

After law school and the death of her fiancé, Brent refocused her career. Ms. Atwater has authored 10 Just Plain Love® Books with more to follow and whose titles are being translated into other languages.

Brent"s mission is to turn the negatives of disease into positives in order to ignite hope and healing within the hearts of her readers.

Ms Atwater is also a pioneer in healing art medicine by scientifically documenting the healing energy, diagnostic abilities and healing benefits of her art for healthcare Paintings That Heal® She is one of the contemporary American painters who are bringing forth a new cultural renaissance by blending her classical artistic training with spirituality and energy infused into her healing art.

Brent Atwater"s Just Plain Love® Books, weekly ASK Brent radio shows, podcasts, blogs, inspiring audience participatory workshops (with awesome demonstrations), upbeat seminars, speaking tours, presentations and consultations bring about transformative and positive results.
Send Q"s to AskBrent@live.com